BELUGA WHALES
AND BABIES
THEIR

MARIANNE JOHNSTON

A Zoo Life Book

The Rosen Publishing Group's
PowerKids Press™
New York

Special thanks to Diane Shapiro of the Bronx Zoo for making this project possible.

Published in 1999 by The Rosen Publishing Group, Inc.
29 East 21st Street, New York, NY 10010

First Edition

Book Design: Resa Listort

Photo Credits: All photos © Wildlife Conservation Society.

Johnston, Marianne.
    Beluga Whales and their babies / by Marianne Johnston.
       p.   cm. — (A Zoo life book)
    Includes index.
    Summary: Describes the characteristics of beluga whales and how mother beluga whales living in aquariums are taught to care for their babies.
    ISBN 0-8239-5315-7
    1.White whale—Juvenile literature. 2. White whale—Infancy—Juvenile literature. 3. Zoo animals—Juvenile literature. [1. White whale. 2. Whales. 3. Animals—Infancy. 4. Zoo animals.]
    I. Title. II. Series: Johnston, Marianne. Zoo life book

QI737.C433C735   1998
599.5'42—dc21   98-18931
                                                                              CIP
                                                                                   AC

Manufactured in the United States of America

CONTENTS

THE BELUGA WHALE

You may have visited an **aquarium** (uh-KWAYR-ee-um) and seen a **beluga** (beh-LOO-guh) whale swimming around a pool. Beluga whales are one of just two **species** (SPEE-sheez) of white whales. Beluga whales can grow to be fifteen feet long and weigh 3,000 pounds, but they are smaller than most other kinds of whales. Unlike most whales, belugas can turn their heads from side to side.

Like all whales, beluga whales are **mammals** (MA-mulz). Most belugas live to be about 25 years old.

ORDER:
CETACEA
FAMILY:
MONODONTIDAE
GENUS & SPECIES:
DELPHINAPTERUS LEUCAS

◀ The beluga whale is a relative of the dolphin and the porpoise.

WHERE DO BELUGA WHALES LIVE?

Beluga whales swim in the icy waters of the Arctic Circle, near the northern part of our planet. They live near the northern shores of lands such as Alaska, Canada, Norway, and Russia. One group of beluga whales lives a little farther south, near the St. Lawrence River in Canada.

In the summer, belugas often travel up rivers. This allows them to enjoy the warmer river waters. Beluga whales have been found hundreds of miles up the Yukon River in Alaska. Most of the time, beluga whales travel in small groups of three to ten whales. In the summer, these whales can be found in groups of over 100.

Here is a healthy beluga. But some belugas are getting sick from pollution in their natural habitats. ▶

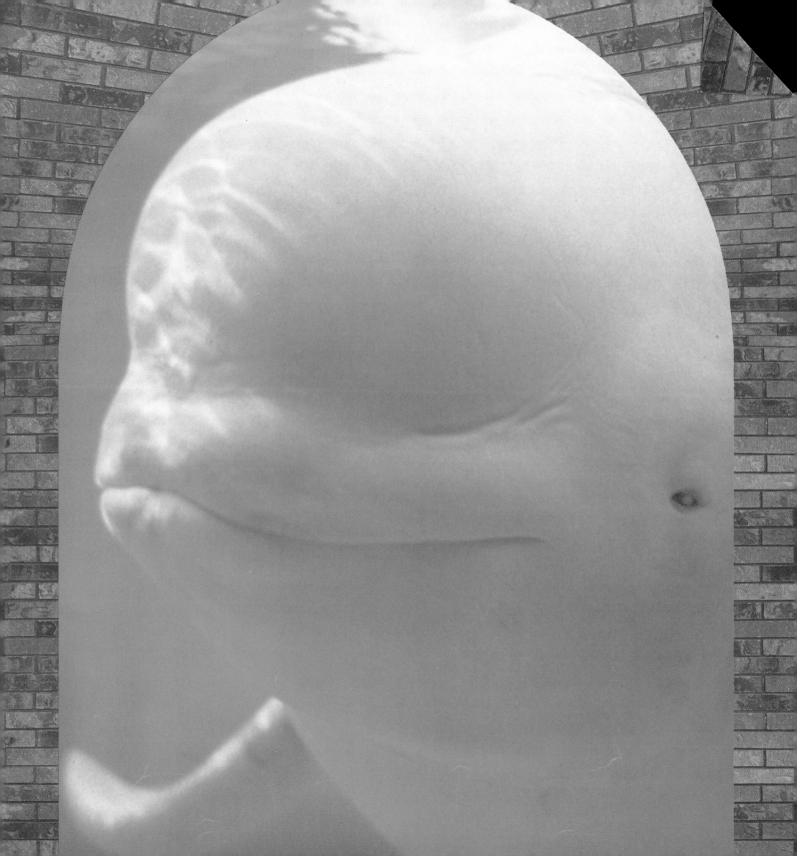

BELUGAS AT THE AQUARIUM

Animals, such as the beluga whale, are often kept in **captivity** (kap-TIH-vih-tee). Scientists may wish to study a beluga whale. Or a sick beluga whale may be taken to an aquarium to get better.

To keep belugas healthy, the water in the aquarium must have the same amount of salt in it as ocean water has. Some aquariums even pump water from the ocean into the aquarium.

In the ocean, beluga whales eat fish. They also eat worms. In aquariums, beluga whales are fed seafood, such as squid. Squid has a lot of water. Beluga whales don't need to drink because they get water from their food.

Some belugas are in captivity, but thousands live in the Arctic waters.

WHEN A BELUGA WHALE IS PREGNANT

One of the most special events at an aquarium is when an animal has a baby. After female beluga whales reach the age of five, they can have babies. Female beluga whales are **pregnant** (PREG-nent) for about fourteen months after they **mate** (MAYT). Human moms are pregnant for only nine months.

To find out if a female beluga whale is pregnant, the aquarium keepers give her a special test. This test is called a **sonogram** (SAH-nuh-gram). The sonogram lets the aquarium keepers see if there is a baby, or **calf** (KAF), inside the female.

Aquarium keepers give all the whales regular health checkups. ▶

A BABY BELUGA ON THE WAY

If a sonogram shows that a beluga whale is pregnant, everyone at an aquarium gets excited. When a beluga whale is pregnant, the aquarium keepers check the whale's blood often. The keepers do this to make sure the mother whale is staying healthy.

When a beluga whale is about to give birth, the keepers must make sure that both the mother and her calf are prepared. The keepers usually move the pregnant beluga to a special pool. This pool cannot be seen by visitors to the aquarium. Excited visitors might bother the **expectant** (ek-SPEK-tent) mother.

◀ The pregnant beluga here is just one day away from giving birth.

13

PREPARING
THE POOL

Most aquarium pools have big windows on the sides so that visitors can see inside. But when a baby is about to be born, those windows need to be covered.

The keepers don't want to confuse the calf. The calf needs to get to the water's surface to take its first breath of air. The keepers cover the windows so that the only light the calf sees is at the water's surface. The calf will then swim easily to the top of the pool.

A mother and baby beluga swim together until the baby grows. ▶

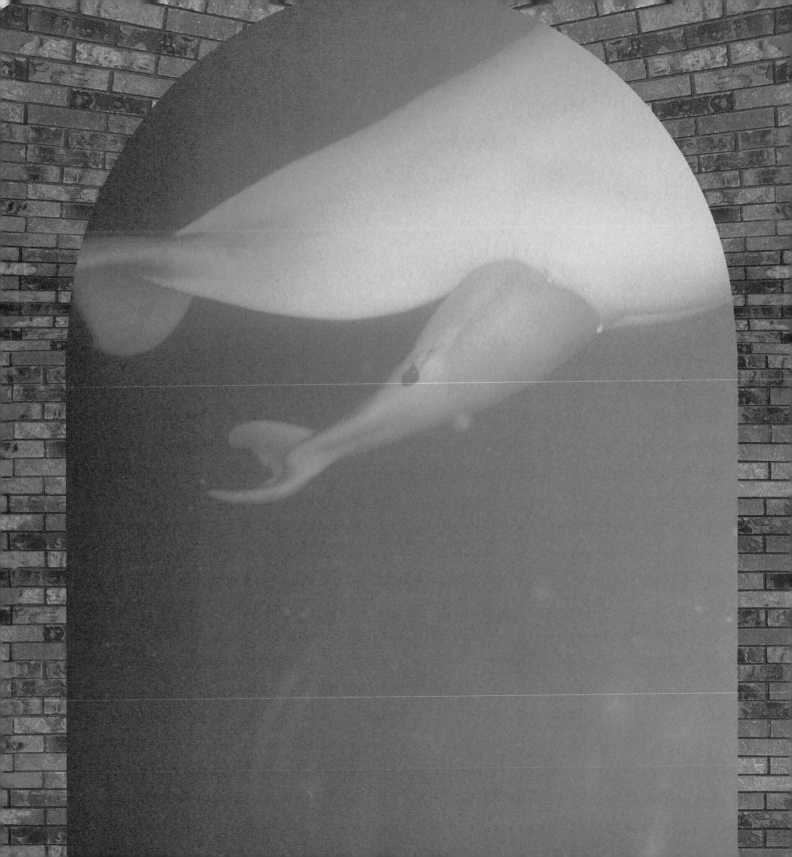

A BELUGA BIRTHDAY

When the keepers have done all they can to prepare for the birth, it is time to sit back and wait. The aquarium keepers watch for a cloud of blood to be released from the back of the female's body. This tells the keepers that the calf will be born soon. For the next ten to twenty hours, the female works hard to bring her calf into the world.

In aquariums, the father whale may be put in the tank with the female while she gives birth.

Finally, after hours of working, the mother whale gives birth to a five-foot-long baby.

Here a beluga is giving birth. The calf is halfway out of the mother's body.

BABY BELUGAS

Even though most full-grown beluga whales are white, beluga calves are usually brown or gray when they are born. By the time the calves are five to eight years old, the young belugas have lost their color and are all white.

For the first two years of life, a baby beluga whale stays very close to its mother. The mother whale watches the calf closely. During these two years, a baby beluga whale will **nurse** (NERS), or drink milk from its mother's body. This is the way most mammals feed their young.

This calf was born in a pool. In the wild, belugas give birth in shallow water that the sun has warmed. ▶

GROWING UP AT THE AQUARIUM

Just like kids, beluga calves love to play. They often chase other whales around the pool. Beluga parents teach their young how to make different sounds. Some of the sounds are chirps, whistles, and squeaks.

Beluga whales are very **smart.** Aquarium keepers teach adult whales many **behaviors** (bee-HAY-vyurz), or tricks. But beluga calves are too young for tricks. Instead, the keepers at the aquarium just spend lots of time playing with the young whales. Balls and surfboards are a few of the things keepers use when playing with calves.

◀ Beluga whales like to have their tongues rubbed.

LEARNING MORE ABOUT WHALES

Before whales were brought to aquariums, many people thought whales were dangerous and scary. Keeping belugas and other whales in captivity allows people to learn more about the whales. Aquarium keepers can also help sick whales that cannot **survive** (ser-VYV) in the wild.

Many whales are **endangered** (en-DAYN-jerd). Luckily, the beluga whale is not endangered. By visiting aquariums, you can help prevent beluga whales from ever becoming **extinct** (ek-STINKT).

WEB SITE

You can learn more about beluga whales at this Web site: http://www.uvm.edu/whale/BelugaWhales.html

GLOSSARY

aquarium (uh-KWAYR-ee-um) A place where beluga whales are kept for study and exhibit.

behavior (bee-HAY-vyur) The things a creature does, including tricks.

beluga (beh-LOO-guh) A Russian word that means "white one."

calf (KAF) A baby whale.

captivity (kap-TIH-vih-tee) Holding at an aquarium.

endangered (en-DAYN-jerd) When something is in danger of no longer existing.

expectant (ek-SPEK-tent) Expecting to give birth.

extinct (ek-STINKT) When a certain kind of animal no longer exists.

mammal (MA-mul) An animal that is warm-blooded, breathes oxygen, and gives birth to live young.

mate (MAYT) A special joining of a male and female body. Afterward, the female may have a baby grow inside her.

nurse (NERS) When a baby drinks milk from its mother's body.

pregnant (PREG-nent) When a female has a baby or babies growing inside her.

sonogram (SAH-nuh-gram) An image produced using sound waves that shows a baby inside its mother.

species (SPEE-sheez) A group of animals that are very much alike.

survive (ser-VYV) To be able to stay alive.

INDEX